Russian Americans

TIFFANY PETERSON

Heinemann Library
Chicago, Illinois

© 2003 Heinemann Library
a division of Reed Elsevier Inc.
Chicago, Illinois

Customer Service 888-454-2279

Visit our website at www.heinemannlibrary.com

Created by the publishing team at Heinemann Library
Designed by Roslyn Broder
Photo Research by Amor Montes de Oca
Printed and Bound in the United States by Lake Book Manufacturing, Inc.

07 06 05 04 03
10 9 8 7 6 5 4 3 2 1

Library of Congress Cataloging-in-Publication Data
Peterson, Tiffany.
    Russian Americans / Tiffany Peterson.
      p. cm. — (We are America)
    Summary: Describes the conditions in Russia that led people
to immigrate to the United States and what their daily lives are
like in their new home.
    Includes bibliographical references (p.) and index.
    ISBN 1-40340-737-1 (lib. bdg.) ISBN 1-40343-138-8 (pbk.)
    1. Russian Americans—Juvenile literature. 2. Immigrants—United States—Juvenile literature.
3. United States—Emigration and immigration—Juvenile literature. 4. Russia (Federation)—
Emigration and immigration—Juvenile literature. 5. Soviet Union
  —Emigration and immigration—Juvenile literature. 6. Russian
  Americans—Biography—Juvenile literature. 7. Immigrants—United States—Biography—Juvenile
literature.   [1. Russian Americans.]   I. Title. II. Series.
    E184.R9P465 2003
    973'.049171—dc21
    2002013101

Acknowledgments
The author and publishers are grateful to the following for permission to reproduce copyright material:
pp. 4, 5, 28, 29 Courtesy of Svetlana Samarina; p. 7 Wolfgang Kaehler/Corbis; p. 8 Stock Montage, Inc.; p. 10 Minnesota Historical Society/Corbis; pp. 11, 13, 18, 21 Bettmann/Corbis; p. 14 Reuters NewMedia Inc./Corbis; p. 15 Alex Brandon/AP Wide World Photo; pp. 16, 17 The Granger Collection; p. 19 Hulton Archive/Getty Images; p. 20 Corbis; p. 22 Hulton-Deutsch Collection/Corbis; p. 23 Kelly Parris/Unicorn Stock Photos L. L. C.; p. 24 Jim Whitner; p. 25 Syracuse Newspapers/Dick Blume/The Image Works; p. 26 Susan Steinkamp/Corbis; p. 27 Robert Holmes/Corbis

Cover photographs by (foreground) Joel Cipes, (background) Corbis

Special thanks to Irina Peris for comments made in preparation of this book.

Some quotations and material used in this book come from the following sources. In some cases, quotes have been abridged for clarity: *Ellis Island Interviews: In Their Own Words* by Peter Morton Coan. New York: Facts on File, 1997; *Teenage Refugees from Russia Speak Out* by Tatyana Zamenova. New York: Rosen Publishing, 1995.

Some words are shown in bold, **like this.** You can find out what they mean by looking in the glossary.

On the cover of this book, a Russian family who moved to Buffalo, New York, is shown in about 1915. In the background, the Russian Hill neighborhood in San Francisco, California, is shown in the late 1800s. A large number of Russians settled in San Francisco.

Contents

One Woman's Story

Svetlana Samarina grew up in a city called Odessa in the **Soviet Union.** Because she was **Jewish,** there were many things in the Soviet Union that were hard for her to do. In the 1970s, when Svetlana was a teenager, several people she knew left the Soviet Union. Svetlana wanted to leave, too. But her parents were afraid to move to the United States. Like many **immigrants,** they did not know what life would be like in America.

At one time, Odessa was ruled by Russia. Russians gave the city its name in 1795. In 1944, Odessa became part of the Soviet Union, like Russia was. Russian leaders formed the Soviet Union in 1922. Today, Odessa is in a country called Ukraine.

Svetlana is shown here on a visit to St. Petersburg, Russia, when she was 14.

At the end of the 1970s, the Samarinas no longer had a choice. Government leaders in the the Soviet Union said no one could leave. But in the late 1980s, people could once again leave the Soviet Union. Svetlana's aunt and uncle went to the United States in 1989. When they left, Svetlana started saving money and planning to follow them. In 1992, Svetlana, her son, and her parents went to San Francisco, California, where Svetlana's aunt and uncle had **settled.**

Svetlana and her son are shown here in 1991, shortly before they moved to San Francisco.

We moved as soon as we had a chance to immigrate here because it's . . . difficult for Russian Jews to get a higher education, good schooling, and good jobs.
—Svetlana Samarina, who immigrated in 1992 when she was 28

Russia

Russia is located east of Europe and north of China. It is the largest country in the world. The land and weather are very different from one part of Russia to another. One section of Siberia, Russia, is the coldest place in the world that people live in. There are also some desert areas in southern Russia. Many different types of people live in Russia. Russia's population includes over 100 different **ethnic** groups.

Moscow is the capital of Russia. Russia is twice the size of Canada. Russia was the largest part of the **Soviet Union.**

This map shows where Russia and the United States are located in the world.

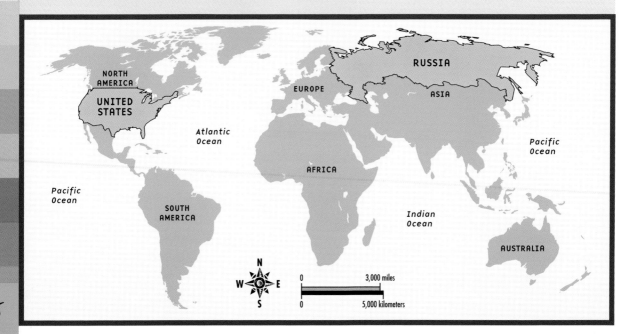

NORTH AMERICA

UNITED STATES

EUROPE

RUSSIA

ASIA

Atlantic Ocean

Pacific Ocean

Pacific Ocean

AFRICA

SOUTH AMERICA

Indian Ocean

AUSTRALIA

N
W E
S

0   3,000 miles

0   5,000 kilometers

*Russians in Alaska built this church in Old Harbor, Alaska, to teach people about their religion, **Russian Orthodoxy.***

The northeast corner of Russia is very close to Alaska. In the 1700s, Russian fur traders hunted in the Aleutian Islands just off the coast of Alaska. These people were adventurers and explorers. They traveled through areas that had not been mapped yet. They were the first Russians to set foot in North America. Alaska was a Russian **colony** until 1867, when the United States bought the land from Russia.

Russian Revolution

For hundreds of years, **czars** were the rulers of Russia. Nicholas II, the last czar of Russia, ruled from 1894 until 1917. A **revolution** in 1917 ended with Nicholas being forced out of power. Vladimir Ilyich Lenin, one of the revolution's leaders, took control of Russia. Under Lenin's rule, Russia became a **communist** country known as the Union of Soviet Socialist Republics, or the **Soviet Union.**

On July 17, 1918, Nicholas II and his entire family were killed. The revolution's leaders wanted neither Nicholas nor anyone from his family to be able to ever rule Russia again.

Time Line

1613–1917	Czars ruled Russia.
1917	Nicholas II steps down and Lenin takes power.
1928	Joseph Stalin takes power and creates a prisonlike atmosphere throughout the Soviet Union.
1941–1945	The United States and the Soviet Union fight together against Germany in **World War Two.**
1945	The **Cold War** begins.
1985	Mikhail Gorbachev creates a more open relationship with the United States.
1991	Soviet Union breaks apart.

By 1922, Russians had lived through years of wars and revolutions. They were worn out, and life seemed to be getting harder. The new government took farms and businesses from the people who owned them. People lost freedoms, such as the freedom of religion. Each family received the same small amount of food from the government. People who spoke out against the new government were arrested and often killed. Many Russian people started looking for places to live a better life, places like the United States.

Russians in the United States

Between 1881 and 1914, about three million people from Russia **immigrated** to the United States. A large number of them were **Jewish.** For hundreds of years in Russia, Jews were treated poorly. Beginning in 1791, Russian Jews were forced to live in an area of western Russia. In 1881, Russian Jews were wrongly blamed for the death of **Czar** Alexander II. Jews were attacked and even killed in **pogroms.** Police and soldiers often stood by without stopping the attacks.

It took about three weeks to get to the United States. This photo shows Russian and Polish immigrants sailing to the United States in about 1905.

Sometimes it took so long for the inspections at Ellis Island that immigrants had to spend the night there. This photo shows immigrants in Ellis Island in 1920.

Many Russian Jews and other Russians decided to move to the United States. They traveled into nearby countries, such as Germany, by train or on foot. There, they boarded ships that took them to New York City. Once they got to New York, immigrants were taken to a place called Ellis Island. There, they went through health checkups and interviews. Inspectors wanted to make sure the immigrants were healthy enough to find jobs. Some sick people were sent back to the country they came from.

More Russian Immigrants

Jews were not the only group treated poorly in Russia. In the 1920s, after the **revolution,** the new government took money, land, and other things owned by wealthy Russians. People who had enough money to pay for the trip left Russia. They moved to Europe, Asia, and the United States.

This map shows the areas in the United States where many Russian people first moved to and where many Russian Americans live today.

Russian Immigration to the United States

These Russian people had to leave Russia in 1923 because they disagreed with the way Russia was being ruled. In Russia, they could have been arrested or even killed because of their beliefs.

People who had money did not necessarily have an easier time coming to the United States. Both wealthy and poor **immigrants** had to go to Ellis Island. They were given health inspections and were questioned

Between 1920 and 1922, about two million people left Russia. About 45,000 came to the United States.

about their plans. Some Americans were afraid that the United States could be taken over by **communists** like Russia had been. If an immigrant was suspected of being a communist, he or she was sent back to Russia.

Later Russian Immigrants

When Joseph Stalin became the leader of the **Soviet Union** in 1929, he announced that Russians could no longer leave the country. But there have been a few periods since then in which Russians were able to **immigrate.** Right after **World War Two,** many Russian soldiers chose not to go back to the Soviet Union. Also, in the 1970s, government leaders allowed some people to leave to be with family members outside the Soviet Union. Many Russians immigrated to the United States at this time.

Mikhail Baryshnikov defected from the Soviet Union in 1974. To defect means to leave your home country to live in another, usually because you don't agree with your own government leaders. Baryshnikov moved to the United States.

This photo shows a neighborhood in Brooklyn, New York, called Brighton Beach. The area has a large Russian-American population.

In 1991, the Soviet Union collapsed. Russians could leave the Soviet Union if they chose. Hundreds of thousands of Russians have immigrated to the United States since then. Most of these recent immigrants have **settled** in New York or California. They find help and support from the Russian Americans in the United States. Like immigrants from other countries, Russian Americans enjoy American **culture.** At the same time, they are proud to be Russian.

Living here for five years, I have learned to love the United States dearly. To me it represents freedom, health, and fun. Of course you have to work hard to earn the freedom and fun you get... but that's what I really like about this country: It gives you so much in return.
—Anastasia, who came to the U.S. in 1989

Living in the United States: The Early Years

Russians who came to the United States from 1890 to 1914 **settled** in many places. Most stayed either near New York City or moved to other big cities like Philadelphia, Pennsylvania, or Chicago, Illinois. Because they came with little or no money, they had to live in areas that were cheap to live in. In New York, they settled in the Lower East Side.

I worked [in a factory] for two weeks and did not like it. The building was eight or ten stories high. The ceilings were very low. The machines were very crowded and dangerous. People were getting hurt every day.

—Harry Germanow, who immigrated from Russia in 1909 when he was eighteen and settled in Philadelphia

Many Russian immigrants settled on the Lower East Side of New York. A street market in that neighborhood is shown in this photo from 1898.

Some Russian boys worked in mines in Pennsylvania, like these shown in 1913.

Few, if any, Russian **immigrants** learned a **trade** before going to the United States. They got jobs in factories and mines. Because they did not already have experience, they were often given the hardest physical jobs. Those who worked in the mines in Pennsylvania rarely saw sunlight and had to breathe dusty air. The dust stuck in their lungs and made them sick. Many of those who stayed in New York City worked in small, crowed shops called sweatshops.

Working in the United States

In the 1920s, wealthy Russians were hurrying to leave the newly formed **Soviet Union.** The government had taken all the things they owned. They had to leave whatever they had in Russia in the rush to get out of the country. This wave of **immigrants** contributed to the United States in general in a variety of ways, as did the earlier immigrants.

Katherine Esau came to the United States after a **revolution** forced her to leave Russia. She wrote a science book about plants that was used in schools all over the world.

Igor Sikorsky came from Russia to New York City in 1919. He invented the world's first helicopter in 1939.

David Sarnoff came to the United States from Russia as a boy in 1900. Later in his life, he built the first radios for people to listen to in their houses. He also helped make the first televisions in the United States.

Some of the jobs that Russian immigrants took included working as professors at universities, teaching music, or translating Russian into English. Some Russians came to the United States to work as inventors, scientists, writers, and musicians. Others came to the United States to write music, such as the famous **composers** Sergei Rachmaninov and Igor Stravinsky.

New Ways of Living

Living and working in the United States was often difficult for Russian **immigrants** at the beginning of the 1900s. But many of them felt safer living in the United States. In Russia, **Jews** had lived in fear of **pogroms.** They were glad to have found a place where they could freely practice their religion. Jewish adults attended religious services on Friday nights. Their children attended schools to learn Hebrew, the language spoken in Jewish religious services.

This photo shows Russian and German immigrants waving American flags in 1903 to welcome United States President Theodore Roosevelt to Victoria, Kansas.

Russian immigrant Jessie Malik worked as a farmer in the United States in the 1930s. She raised chickens in Lakewood, New Jersey.

Once they had **settled** in the United States, some Russian teenagers wanted to break away from some of the old Russian **traditions.** For some families in Russia, it was common for parents to arrange marriages for their children. In the early 1900s in the United States, however, young Russian immigrants wanted to be more American. They wanted to wear American clothes, speak English, and choose their own future husbands and wives.

Seeing the Statue of Liberty. It was thrilling to know we had arrived and would soon be on land.
—Betty Garoff, who went to the U.S. from Russia in 1921, when she was eight

Culture and Celebrations

Today, Russian **traditions** and **culture** are still a part of Russian-American life. Weddings, for example, are usually long, joyous celebrations with a lot of food, singing, and dancing. During the wedding, the bride and groom are given a loaf of bread. The bread is supposed to represent that the couple will always have enough to eat. This tradition is also sometimes used for Russian Americans who have just moved into a new home or who are visiting friends or family.

*A **Russian Orthodox** wedding service in 1946 is shown in this photo. In this type of service, crowns are held over the heads of the people getting married.*

These women and men dancers are from an area that used to be part of the Soviet Union. They performed a traditional dance in a parade in North Carolina in 2001.

At some Russian weddings and other events, guests perform traditional dances. One famous dance is called the *kazachok*. It is named for Russian soldiers who were famous for their skill at riding horses. The dance is performed by groups of men, often in a straight line. They dance, jump, and kick out their legs, all from a squatting position.

Traditional Russian dances are performed to music played on the accordion or the *balalaika*—a small, stringed instrument similar to a guitar.

Families and Schools

Russian-American family members are often very friendly, close, and supportive of one another. Some older people live with their children's families. Family members and relatives support one another with money and care. For **immigrant** families, keeping some of these family **traditions** is difficult since many American adults live in different states than their parents.

My family is very close. That's the way it's always been. If my brother or I have problems, we always go to our family because these people understand us and know how to help. . . I love my family, and I miss them when I don't see them. I can't live without them.

—Marianna, who immigrated from Russia in the 1990s

This family came to Chicago to escape violence and danger in Russia in the 1990s.

Russian Vova Sharapov got to study in the United States for about a month in 2000. He is shown reading an article about basketball star Michael Jordan.

Russian-American parents encourage their children to study hard and do well in school. In Russia in the early 1900s, many children left school early to work for their parents. Today, Russian-American students go to school all the way through high school. And most go on to study in colleges.

Russian-American Contributions

Russian **immigrants** have made many contributions to the United States and American **culture**. One of the things Russian Jews brought was the Yiddish language. Yiddish words have made their way into American English, as have some Russian words.

Words and Phrases from Russian Immigrants

Yiddish word	Meaning
Mazel tov!	Congratulations!
Oy gevald!	Oh no!
chutzpah	nerve

Russian word	Meaning
babushka	older Russian woman
sputnik	satellite

Mstislav Rostropovich played the cello for United States President George Bush in 1989.

Russian food is also available in many cities throughout the United States. There was even a Russian fast-food restaurant, Rush'n Express, in Yorkville, New York.

Russian-American musicians and writers have also made great contributions to art and entertainment. Musicians Mstislav Rostropovich and Vladimir Horowitz are known worldwide. People all over the world have heard the works of Russian-American **composer** Irving Berlin.

One Woman's Story: Svetlana in the United States

This is a photo of Svetlana and her husband, Uri. They met shortly after Svetlana came to the United States.

Like many **immigrants,** Svetlana thinks that one of the hardest parts of immigrating was not knowing English. She went to a group that helped immigrants get started in the United States. Svetlana was able to take English classes and learn the skills she needed to get a job. It was very important that Svetlana be able to find a good job. Her parents were in their sixties and did not speak English. They could not find jobs. Svetlana took care of the whole family.

Svetlana's son was shy when they arrived in the United States. Once he started kindergarten, however, he quickly learned English and made new friends. But Svetlana still wants her son to continue speaking Russian so he can be close to his grandparents. They are all Americans now, but like many immigrants, Svetlana wants her son to remember where his family is from originally.

Svetlana feels lucky she had a chance to move to the United States. Today, she is a U.S. citizen.

Russian Immigration Chart

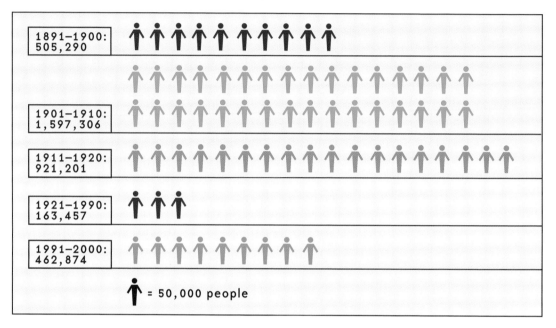

1891–1900: 505,290	👤👤👤👤👤👤👤👤👤👤
1901–1910: 1,597,306	👤👤👤👤👤👤👤👤👤👤👤👤👤👤👤👤 👤👤👤👤👤👤👤👤👤👤👤👤👤👤👤👤
1911–1920: 921,201	👤👤👤👤👤👤👤👤👤👤👤👤👤👤👤👤👤👤
1921–1990: 163,457	👤👤👤
1991–2000: 462,874	👤👤👤👤👤👤👤👤👤

👤 = 50,000 people

*From 1820 to 2000, about 3,906,580 people came to the United States from Russia and the **Soviet Union.***

Source: U.S. Immigration and Naturalization Service

More Books to Read

Bierman, Carol. *Journey to Ellis Island: How My Father Came to America.* New York: Hyperion Books, 1998.

Haberle, Susan E. *Jewish Immigrants.* Mankato, Minn.: Blue Earth Books, 2003.

Toht, Patricia. *Daily Life in Ancient and Modern Moscow.* Minneapolis, Minn.: Runestone Press, 2000.

Glossary

Cold War period between World War Two and 1990 in which the Soviet Union and the United States tried to be more powerful than each other

colony territory that is owned or ruled by another country

communist person or government that supports communism, a political system in which there is one party and government owns all factories, natural resources, and goods

composer someone who writes music for others to sing or play

culture ideas, skills, arts, and way of life for a certain group of people

czar ruler of Russia until the revolution in 1917. A czar was similar to a king.

ethnic of or about races or large groups of people who have the same customs and characteristics

immigrate to come to a country to live there for a long time. A person who immigrates is an immigrant.

Jew someone who follows the Jewish religion or has Jewish ancestors

pogrom violent attack against Jewish people. A large number of Jewish people were killed during pogroms in Russia.

revolution fight to change the ways a country's rulers act

Russian Orthodoxy branch of Christian religion that started in Russia

settle to make a home for yourself and others

Soviet Union large country made up of fifteen smaller republics, the largest of which was Russia. The Soviet Union existed from 1922 to 1991.

trade person's job that requires training. Making things out of silver and making musical instruments are both trades.

tradition belief or practice that has been passed through the years from one generation to the next

World War Two war fought from 1939 to 1945 by Germany, Japan, and Italy on one side and the United States, Great Britain, China, Poland, France, and the Soviet Union on the other.

Index